Latin America's Journey to the Market
From Macroeconomic Shocks to Institutional Therapy

Moisés Naím

An International Center for Economic Growth Publication

ICS Press
San Francisco, California

Publication of this Occasional Paper was funded by the United States Agency for International Development.

Inquiries, book orders, and catalog requests should be addressed to ICS Press, 720 Market Street, San Francisco, California 94102, USA. Telephone: (415) 981-5353; fax: (415) 986-4878; book orders toll free within the contiguous United States: (800) 326-0263.

Library of Congress Cataloging-in-Publication Data

to come

ISBN: 1-55815-457-4

TABLE OF CONTENTS

Preface v

Introduction 1

Box 1: Privatization: Still Far to Go 3

The Stages of Economic Liberalization 4

From Macroeconomic Shock Therapy to Institutional Chemotherapy 8

Chart 1: Goals, Targets, and Institutional Challenges 10

Chart 2: Actors, Impacts, and Political Costs 12

The Roots of State Incapacity 13

The Decline of the Latin American State: Statistics, Anecdotes, and Comparisons 17

Box 2: Wages of Sin: The Collapse of Government Salaries in Latin America 27

Box 3: "If You Pay Peanuts, You'll Get Monkeys for Your Ministers" 30

Box 4: Here Today, Gone Tomorrow: Latin America's Ministerial Turnover 31

What to Do? Where to Begin? 34

Appendix 41

Notes 43

PREFACE

We are pleased to publish this essay by Moisés Naím on *Latin America's Journey to the Market: From Macroeconomic Shocks to Institutional Therapy* as the sixty-second in our series of Occasional Papers. The series features reflections on broad policy issues by noted policy makers and scholars.

Dr. Naím addresses an important issue for Latin American countries that have turned away from direct state economic management and are enjoying strong economic performance as a result of their turn to the market. He argues that even in countries that have gone furthest toward the market, the state continues to perform functions that would be better performed by the private sector, while failing to perform basic services that the state must provide in a strong market economy.

Dr. Naím argues that most of the Latin American reforms today were implemented by executive orders that changed the macroeconomic environment. They were not implemented and sustained by reforms that depended on the ongoing performance of administrative agencies.

The author argues that the challenge for Latin America today is to rediscover the state. The failure to meet this challenge will threaten the region's economic and political stability, with its fragile democracies.

Dr. Naím is currently a senior associate at the Carnegie Endowment in Washington, D.C., where he is also director of its Latin American programs. He has studied these issues in his positions as both a government minister (of industry in the Venezuelan government) and as an executive director in the World Bank.

We think that Dr. Naím's message is extremely important for many Latin American governments at the present time. His narrative is also important for countries in other regions, struggling to move away from government management of economies and toward the market, while building strong government capacities to perform the core institutional functions on which market economies depend.

Nicholas Ardito-Barletta
General Director
International Center for Economic Growth

Panama City, Panama
December 1994

ABOUT THE AUTHOR

Moisés Naím is a senior associate at the Carnegie Endowment in Washington, D.C. where he is also the director of its Latin American programs. Naím's research centers on the management of economic policy changes and on issues of trade and investment in developing countries with special reference to Latin America. He is the author or editor of five books, numerous academic articles, and writes frequently for newspapers and magazines in the United States and Latin America.

Educated at the Massachusetts Institute of Technology, Dr. Naím served as Venezuela's Minister of Industry and as an executive director at the World Bank. He is currently a member of the United States Academy of Science/National Research Council's Committee on Democracy and States in Transition, of the Editorial Board of *The Latin American Research Review,* of the World Bank's Latin American advisory board and a Fellow of the World Economic Forum in Geneva as well as a member of the board of several private corporations and nonprofit institutions. He teaches at The Johns Hopkins School of Advanced International Studies in Washington and at IESA in Caracas.

MOISÉS NAÍM

Latin America's Journey to the Market
From Macroeconomic Shocks to Institutional Therapy

Introduction

At the end of this century, in Latin America, like almost everywhere else, few institutions are held in more disrepute than the state. The state is widely perceived as too incompetent, too corrupt, or too crippled by political restrictions to be a reliable or effective instrument with which to achieve collective objectives. Hence, the turn to the market.

Discovering the market and abandoning overreliance on the state has done wonders for Latin America. In the 1980s, average inflation for the region was more than 150 percent per year; as recently

The research on which this essay is based was made possible by the Carnegie Endowment for International Peace and the Inter-American Dialogue. An abridged version of this paper was published in the Fall 1994 issue of the *Journal of Democracy*. My sincere thanks to Zan Northrip for his enormous and intelligent help with the collection and processing of most of the data presented here and to Deborah Hudson for her able assistance. I am, however, solely responsible for errors and omissions in the text.

as 1990, prices were rising by 1,200 percent annually. By 1993, inflation had plummeted to 19 percent, and economies that had shrunk every year for more than a decade had reestablished patterns of growth.[1] While average growth in the region is not high, some countries, such as Chile and Argentina, achieved growth rates that in some years put them on a par with the economic powerhouses of East Asia. A region where, for years, any excess funds instantly became flight capital is now a powerful magnet for international investment. Latin America is attracting foreign capital to the tune of more than US$50 billion per year, eight times more per year than in the 1980s and twice what it used to attract before it lost its creditworthiness in 1982. About half of these inflows are going to the region's international reserves, which despite trade deficits—partly related to the removal of import barriers—reached US$92 billion in 1992, the highest level in this century.

But the discovery of the market will soon force Latin American countries to rediscover the state. Sustaining and deepening the positive changes brought about by the turn to the market will require states to increase their technical and managerial capacities far beyond present levels. In most countries of the region, even those that have advanced farthest in the adoption of market reforms, the state continues to perform functions better suited for the private sector while exhibiting an appalling incompetence in discharging core public functions. The process of dismantling the state and limiting its scope of intervention is still far from finished, and many more market reforms are pending (see Box 1 for a look at the extent of Latin American privatization). At the same time, however, the more difficult task of creating or rehabilitating indispensable public-sector institutions lags far behind the requirements of both the new economic strategy and the political imperatives imposed by Latin America's feeble democracies.[2] While the region's political instability may be attributed to a variety of causes, it has been exacerbated in recent years by the inability of the state to deliver basic public services. Together with the social effects of high inflation and unemployment, the acute deterioration of state capacity has become a powerful destabilizing force.

Box 1
Privatization: Still Far to Go

Actual progress in Latin American privatization has failed to live up to the common assumption of withering public enterprise. The same can be said of privatizations in other parts of the globe. Except in a few countries, privatization programs seem to have generated more publicity than actual transactions. In fact, rather than changing hands or simply stagnating, recent research shows that Latin America's public enterprises generated a greater portion of GDP from 1986 to 1991 than they did from 1978 to 1985.

While public enterprises' share of total employment and total investment both fell, their larger role in GDP comes as a shock. The conventional wisdom is that their impact shrank markedly with the global fire sale of state assets.

But the world's privatizations have been concentrated in a very few countries and sectors. Of the 6,832 transactions executed by 1992, two-thirds were sales of (formerly) East German enterprises. Mexico and Chile took second and third place, respectively, but their programs far outpaced those seen in other Latin American countries. Argentina joined the ranks of large divestors by privatizing nearly everything in 1993, one year beyond the scope of this study.

For now, however, public enterprises remain major players in Latin American economies. Those privatizations that grabbed headlines over the past decade were generally the easier ones. Many of those that remain will have complex preconditions to divestment, putting the political and technical capacities of owner governments to a difficult test. Skillful salesmanship on the part of governments will also be needed as less attractive assets come to market.

Latin American public enterprise has stayed bigger than you think . . .
Public Enterprise Value Added as Percentage of GDP, 1978–91

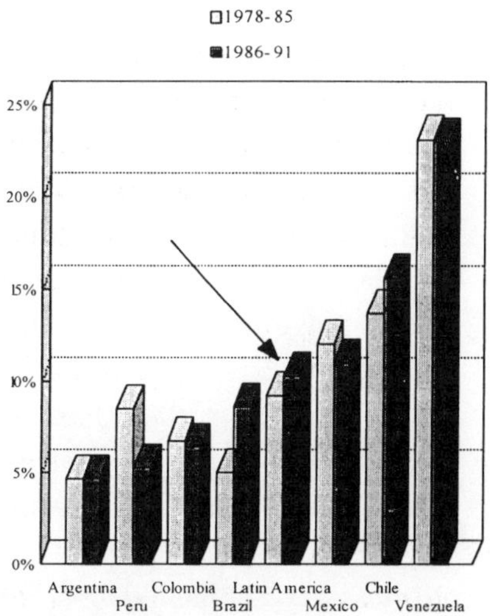

Source: Ahmed Galal.

And the region's privatizations have been concentrated in very few countries.
Global Privatizations Through 1992

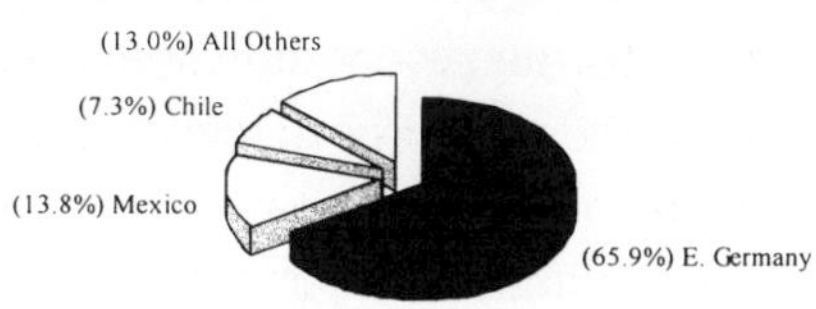

Source: Kikeri, Nellis and Shirley, "Privatization: Lessons of Experience," World Bank, 1992.

Source: Ahmed Galal, "Extent, Performance and Reform of Public Enterprise: A Comparative Analysis," December 1993 (draft chapter for forthcoming World Bank Policy Research Report, *The Changing Role of the State: Strategies for Reforming Public Enterprises*).

The biggest threats to economic stability—a relapse into fiscal disarray and insufficient international competitiveness—also flow from the failure to improve the performance of existing public institutions and policies. Sluggishness in creating new public agencies that are critical for the functioning of an open, market-based economy is undermining economic performance. Moreover, unless the administrative capacity of Latin American governments is increased, social conditions are bound to deteriorate, regardless of how much money is poured into social programs. Bringing the state back in ways that support and reinforce recent progress—without restoring the tendency to inflict economic, social, and moral havoc that the state has exhibited in the past—will be the central challenge facing governments throughout the region.

The spectacular turnaround Latin America has witnessed so far did not hinge on the ongoing performance of public agencies. Rather, executive orders altering the macroeconomic environment did most of the work. That stage is over. Most countries are now entering a new stage in which they must respond to different priorities under political, institutional, and international circumstances that differ markedly from those that characterized the period in which market reforms were launched.

The Stages of Economic Liberalization

Latin America's recent progress was achieved by shrinking the state and rejecting economic policies that depended on the discretionary decisions of poorly trained bureaucrats accountable only to the political bosses who controlled their badly paid but highly profitable public jobs. Countries dismantled some of the most pernicious public institutions. Agencies in charge of policing compliance with thousands of officially set prices, of administering foreign-exchange controls and trade quotas, and of screening and evaluating foreign investment proposals, for example, were done away with. Entire divisions within ministries were idled by the new policies. The adoption of a stern fiscal discipline to reduce the swelling of public budgets, the widespread deregulation of trade and investment, and the privatization of some money-losing state-owned enterprises also contributed to an increase in price stability and the restoration of growth.

All of these measures had three characteristics in common: First, the initial reform decisions centered mostly on changing the rules that determined macroeconomic behavior. Second, macroeconomic reforms could be adopted by the executive branch in relative isolation from the rest of the political system and were administratively simple to execute. Third, the new policies implied the *dismantling* of many existing agencies, and did not require their immediate *replacement* with other organizations.

In other words, other than issuing decrees or executive orders enacting the new policies and reassigning the staff of eliminated agencies to other public-sector jobs, governments generally did not have to worry about creating new organizations to replace the old ones. Thus, in the last ten years or so, Latin America has witnessed a massive process of deliberate—often positive—institutional dismantling. Nonetheless, with the exception of Chile, and possibly Costa Rica, the dismantling of state organizations was accompanied by the unintended and profound operational deterioration of indispensable public agencies. Although this deterioration had been going on for decades, it was accelerated first by the fiscal collapse provoked by the debt crisis and, more recently, by the drastic budget cuts needed to shrink the fiscal deficit. These wholesale budget cuts often left agencies without any realistic possibility of recruiting or retaining essential technical personnel or of procuring other needed resources. Essentially, public-sector institution building in Latin America has been either neglected or impaired by lack of interest, money, and administrative capacity. While this neglect has been a chronic problem, it has now reached levels that, unless corrected, will threaten both democracy and economic stability.

Three broad factors created the conditions for the virtual abandonment of the state in the 1980s. The imperative to reduce public spending converged with a soaring enthusiasm among Latin American elites about market solutions and a growing public disgust with state ineffectiveness, waste, and corruption. These three factors nurtured an environment in which any initiative aimed at strengthening the public sector had to overcome daunting obstacles. The Latin American state was never very effective to begin with, and decades of decay have left it with few friends.

Other factors also impaired the functioning of the state. Paradoxically, the trend toward regional decentralization, which has been accelerated by the political dynamics of democratization, has worsened the organizational crisis of the public sector. The paradox is that in the long run, political and administrative decentralization offers the only hope for the improvement of certain public services that are better managed and monitored at the local level. In the short run, however, the decentralization process frequently has led to a decline in the performance of the public sector. Hastily improvised decisions and political pressures have suddenly burdened the meager administrative capabilities of state and local governments with tasks that they are unable to perform properly, if at all. Decentralization has also added to the complexities of managing the federal government. The fiscal problems of Brazil and Argentina, for example, are closely related to the disarray of public finances in autonomous regions, and the delivery of health care and education in many countries suffers from excessive institutional fragmentation and weak local agencies. Colombia's courageous fight against narco-terrorism is made more difficult by the ease with which drug lords can gain political control of weak local governments that have been made even more vulnerable by a well-intentioned but destabilizing decentralization process.

The creation and development of the institutions needed to support the new economic policies (such as regulatory agencies, antitrust and antidumping commissions, export promotion bodies, consumer protection agencies, social safety-net organizations, and so on) will be slow, cumbersome, expensive, and technically difficult. Even more challenging will be the upgrading of existing public agencies devastated by decades of neglect, underinvestment, and capture by special interests. Furthermore, the significant political autonomy and presidential authority that characterized governmental decision making in the first wave of reforms that swept the region will be hard to maintain in the future.

With the exceptions of Chile and Mexico, Latin America's economic reforms were launched in the political context of competitive, multiparty democracies. Nonetheless, presidents and technocratic economic cabinets were able to design and implement changes in macroeconomic rules with relatively little interference from the rest of the political system or the public sector.[3] In most countries, the institutional and legal steps needed to launch a radical macroeconomic overhaul tended to be technically simple and often fell under the authority of the executive branch. Where that was not the case, the prospect of acute crisis and imminent economic debacle usually helped presidents secure extraordinary legal authority. Such authority enabled them to adopt economic emergency measures that would otherwise have required congressional ratification.

That was the case in Bolivia in 1985, in Argentina at the beginning of President Carlos Menem's term, in Brazil when President Fernando Collor took office with inflation running at 80 percent per month, and in Venezuela during the interim government of President Ramón Velazquez, who replaced ousted President Carlos Perez. In other cases—Chile after Pinochet, Honduras, Guatemala, Costa Rica—presidents were able to build temporary political coalitions that allowed them to pursue their reform plans within the framework of the constitution. In contrast, Peruvian president Alberto Fujimori—with the backing of the army—abolished congress and the courts in 1992 and proceeded to govern by decree. This increased political control enabled the government to pass important economic reforms that had been fiercely resisted by a congress dominated by the opposition.

For the most part, then, Latin American macroeconomic reforms were adopted with little participation and influence from congress, the judiciary, regional and state authorities, public-sector unions, the public bureaucracy, and other significant actors.[4] Reforms were often formulated and decided by a small group formed by the president, a finance minister who acted as the "economic czar," and the governor of the central bank. The "dismantling" nature of the initial decisions made it easier to formulate and adopt these reforms with a significant degree of political autonomy. Launching market-oriented economic-stabilization reform programs requires a lot of courage, and entails immense risks and huge political costs. Once the reforms are decided on, however, their execution is relatively simple—particularly compared to the institutional reconstruction that must follow the initial macroeconomic changes if stability is to be maintained.

From Macroeconomic Shock Therapy to Institutional Chemotherapy

The era of decree-driven, hard-to-decide but simple-to-execute macroeconomic shocks is mostly over. Now, in the mid-1990s, Latin America is entering a new stage in its reform process. Shock therapy is giving way to a much slower, more unpredictable, and generally more difficult stage of institutional creation and rehabilitation. Massive and painful macroeconomic surgery was indispensable to save the patient. Institutional therapy—protracted, equally painful, and much more complex—is required to give the patient a chance to live without the debilitating threat of relapses into the economic and political illnesses that made drastic macroeconomic corrections necessary.

In this new stage, governments will have to do much more than ensure that macroeconomic stability is maintained and that attractive conditions for competitive private investment are created. While striving to maintain a still precarious macroeconomic equilibrium, they will also have to concentrate on building the organizational infrastructure of the state and tend to a potentially explosive social situation. The pending agenda in Latin America is overwhelming, both because the list of tasks is long and because the needed changes are technically, politically, and administratively complicated. Governments will have to move swiftly to overhaul the financing, production, and distribution of public services in many areas: education, health care, transportation, justice, and personal safety, to name a few. Privatization will have to go beyond airlines and hotels and extend to infrastructure, utilities, social services, mining, and oil. Tax collection, banking supervision, regulation of privatized monopolies, social security, labor practices, export promotion, the civil service, the judiciary, and a plethora of other areas are in dire need of more and better governmental attention. The requirements in terms of statecraft, political maneuvering, and managerial talent of these "Stage II" reforms are immense. In countries that have stepped into this second stage, the political insulation of decision making that characterized the initial reforms has already been replaced with a numbing cacophony of voices of those scrambling to influence the next phase of reform in Latin America.

Furthermore, in many countries, the transition from Stage I to Stage II also coincides with complex political adjustments associated with the transformation of incipient, far-from-consolidated democratic regimes.[5] Chart 1 presents a comparative synthesis of the main goals, reform targets, actors, and institutional challenges that lie ahead.

The central message of Chart 1 is that, while in the launching phase of economic liberalization much could be achieved even with a highly ineffective state, market reforms will be impossible to consolidate if the performance of public institutions is not dramatically improved. The fact that such improvements are inherently slow has important implications for the sequence that reform efforts are exhibiting.

Recent experience in Latin America and elsewhere shows the importance of noneconomic imperatives in defining the sequence of specific reforms. The notion that the economy needs to be stabilized in order to facilitate the adoption of other structural changes has guided economic reform in many countries, and for good reasons.[6] But a pattern is now emerging in which, shortly after launching stabilization measures, governments tend to enact *some* structural reforms and not others. For example, most countries have been able to reform their trade regime, open the stock market, and privatize airlines and hotels. Very few, however, have been able to modernize their labor legislation, restructure higher education, or privatize state-owned companies in resource-based sectors where international competitiveness and political symbolism are high (for example, copper in Chile and oil in Venezuela and Mexico). While economic crises may, under some circumstances, force the adoption of some of the structural changes, other important determinants are: 1) the political power of the specific groups affected by the reforms to resist, stall, or derail them; 2) the legal authority the central government has unilaterally to impose the reforms; and 3) the administrative capacity to execute the reforms.[7]

In Stage I, then, economic-stabilization measures dominate the public agenda but some structural changes are implemented as well (see Chart 1). In Stage II, structural changes take preeminence. Yet, the tardiness with which crucial structural changes are adopted and their paucity of results often lead to the reemergence of macroeconomic

Chart 1
Goals, Targets, and Institutional Challenges

	Stage I	Stage II
PRIORITIES	• Reduce inflation • Restore growth	• Improve social conditions • Increase international competitiveness • Maintain macroeconomic stability
REFORM STRATEGY	• Change macroeconomic rules • Reduce size and scope of state • Dismantle institutions of protectionism and statism	• Create and rehabilitate institutions • Boost competitiveness of the private sector • Reform production, financing, and delivery of healthcare, education, and other public services • Create the "economic institutions of capitalism" • Build new "international economic insertion"
TYPICAL INSTRUMENTS (Reform Targets)	• Drastic budget cuts and tax reform • Price liberalization (including exchange and interest rates) • Trade and foreign investment liberalization • Private-sector deregulation • Creation of social "emergency funds" bypassing social ministries • "Easier" privatizations (hotels, airlines, some manufacturing)	• Reform of labor legislation and practices • Civil-sector reform • Restructuring of government, especially social ministries • Overhaul of administration of justice • Upgrade of regulatory capacities (for privatized utilities and other monopolies, antitrust, antidumping, financial sector, environment, labor, etc.) • Improvement of tax-collection capabilities • Sectoral conversion and restructuring (industry, agriculture, banking, services, mining, etc.) • "Complex" Privatizations (infrastruture, utilities, mining, public services) • Building of export promotion capacities • Restructuring of relations between states and federal government

imbalances, which require Stage I-like macroeconomic corrections (such as sudden fiscal adjustments or currency devaluations), albeit not as radical as those that characterized the initial reform program. Thus stabilization and structural change take place in both stages of the reform process.

A very important distinction between the two stages is that after the initial macroeconomic reforms are adopted, most countries enter a period in which a larger number of actors begin to participate, making the internal logic and technical consistency of the policies much more vulnerable to the impact of political compromises, contradictions, and institutional failures. Bypassing or ignoring the entrenched and defensive public bureaucracy—a luxury frequently enjoyed by the government teams that launch initial reform measures—is more difficult in this stage. In contrast with the policy changes characteristic of Stage I, the costs of institutional changes are heavily concentrated in specific groups likely to lose permanently the advantages and privileges they traditionally enjoyed. The price surges that come in the wake of a currency devaluation or the tightening of monetary policy are not targeted at any single group and in theory, if not always in practice, are temporary. But layoffs in a privatized steel mill and the elimination of farm subsidies are both permanent changes with costs shouldered by specific groups. The groups immediately affected by specific reforms are easier to mobilize politically than the widely dispersed segments of society that bear the initial burden of macroeconomic adjustment. In general, it is easier to organize a public march by university students, hospital workers, or farmers than by those who suffer the consequences of a currency devaluation or an interest-rate hike. Chart 2 presents a comparative synthesis of principal actors, impacts, and political costs associated with the transition from Stage I to Stage II of the reform process. The fear of imminent economic catastrophe was the fundamental motivation for Stage I reforms. Stage II reforms require the more elusive motivation of a broad national consensus about the general direction of economic and social policies.

The pending reform agenda for governments throughout the region has as its common denominator the need for sophisticated public management in a context of growing, and sometimes extreme,

Chart 2
Actors, Impacts, and Political Costs

	Stage I	Stage II
PRINCIPAL ACTORS	• Presidency • Economic cabinet • Central banks • Multilateral financial institutions • Private financial groups and foreign portfolio investors	• Presidency and cabinet • Congress • Public bureaucracy • The judiciary • Unions • Political parties • The media • State and local governments • The private sector
PUBLIC IMPACT OF REFORMS	• Immediate • High public visibility	• Medium-term and long-term • Low public visibility
TECHNICAL AND ADMINISTRATIVE COMPLEXITY OF REFORMS	• Moderate to low	• Very high
NATURE OF POLITICAL COSTS	• "Temporary corrections" widely distributed among the population	• Permanent elimination of special advantages for specific groups
MAIN GOVERNMENTAL CHALLENGE	• Macroeconomic management by insulated technocratic elites	• Institutional development highly dependent on mid-level public-sector management

politicization and reform fatigue. The tasks ahead depend on cohesive state action, whether in the building of reliable social security systems or in the development of regulatory frameworks that increase confidence in the local stock market, whether in the restructuring of hospitals or in the overhaul of the judiciary. The heroes of the next wave of reform will not be a handful of powerful technocrats well versed in the complexities of macroeconomic management. Rather, they will be a myriad of mid-level public managers adroitly building the indispensable organizational structures required to run the state. Though not as glamorous or visible as unleashing the market with a few decrees, this slow and unwieldy organizational construction must become a central preoccupation of governments set on consolidating economic liberalization and political stability. Clearly, market-based solutions can be effectively utilized to boost or minimize the involvement of the state in the execution of these Stage II reforms. Without the intense utilization of public agencies, however, the stability of market reforms will be jeopardized. Unfortunately, the public agencies that must be utilized are either non-existent or plagued by corruption, incompetence, and congestion.

The Roots of State Incapacity

The state in Latin America does not work. Though state capacity may have been better developed during limited periods in certain countries, in most of them, the state has never worked properly. Historians stress the legacy of inadequate institutions, legal codes, and political structures left by the Iberian conquest and colonialism. Political scientists have shown that the poor performance of the Latin American state reflects a distribution of economic and political power that biases public action in favor of the rich, squeezes the middle class, and excludes the poor. Government agencies "captured" by special interests lack the autonomy to formulate and execute policies that benefit the general population and instead serve the narrow interests of the small groups of elites that control them. Latin American governments have traditionally exhibited a dismal capacity for preventing the interests of small groups and even families or individuals from taking precedence over the public interest. Peter Evans contrasts this "predatory state," which is also typical of Africa, with what he calls the "developmental state" that is more common in East Asian countries. As he notes, the "developmental state"

> engenders a more meritocratic civil service and long term career rewards that heighten commitment and create a sense of corporate coherence within the state that, in turn, become a major source of autonomy. . . . [By contrast, in predatory states] the civil service becomes either a second-best option for the risk averse or a temporary exercise in diversification for what are really private sector careers.[8]

Evans also stresses that the developmental state is not insulated from society but is embedded in a concrete set of social ties that binds the state to society and provides institutionalized channels for the continuous negotiation of goals and policies. Developmental states, then, both are well embedded in society and retain a substantial degree of autonomy from special interests.

What causes some states to become "developmental" while others continue to exhibit "predatory" behavior remains a mystery. Clearly, though, predatory states and high levels of inequality in income and wealth go hand in hand. The policies of predatory states tend to increase inequality, which in turn facilitates the capture of the state by the groups in which wealth and power are concentrated. It is perhaps no accident that Latin America, with its long tradition of ineffectual public action, has always exhibited the most inequitable income distribution in the world.

The voracity of plundering elites is not the only factor impairing the effectiveness of state action. Another classic explanation for state underperformance is the rapid growth of populations and their expectations. These variables grow much faster than does the financial and institutional capacity of the state to accommodate them, thus condemning the state apparatus to be constantly overwhelmed by demands. A variation of this vicious circle is evident in Latin America's recent past. Public policies adopted to assuage popular frustration and proclaimed to help the poor often led to dismal economic performance, an overextended public sector, unsustainable foreign indebtedness, and, eventually, the bankruptcy of public finances, more poverty, and even greater inequality.

The chronic failure to alleviate poverty has enormously increased the burden on all public agencies by forcing them to take on emergency welfare functions, which has only served to undermine their performance even further. Public employment became the preferred instrument for dealing with chronic unemployment or nonexistent social safety nets. Those familiar with the inner workings of Latin American public bureaucracies know that discharging the formal functions that justify an agency's existence weighs much less in determining its daily operations than does the need to serve as a welfare agency for its employees and their families. Often this is their tacit, but dominant, organizational mission. For example, the Ministry of Education—usually the largest employer in the country—is as much a distribution channel of public resources to its employees as it is a supplier of educational services to the population. The same holds for ministries of health, agriculture, labor, public works, and even the armed forces—not to mention, of course, state-owned enterprises. In many countries, the problems related to the provision of clothing, meals, transportation, or medical services to the employees of a given ministry often command as much attention from its top officials—and consume as much of its budget—as the statutory tasks of the agency. The same can be said of Latin American social security systems. Their administrative costs—mostly the wage bill—are the highest in the world.[9] Even the social security system is as much a means to transfer resources to its employees as it is a mechanism to serve the outside clients that justify its existence. Naturally, this spurs other public agencies to develop their own social security systems for their employees, sometimes at the expense of services for those who do not have access to a public job. In this way, nonexistent or ineffectual social safety nets create demands on public agencies that make accomplishing their mission nearly impossible. Currently, very few public agencies in the region are capable of attaining their purported goals.

Political patronage, clientelism, and the other classic forms of mismanagement common to all public sectors are, of course, prevalent and deeply ingrained in Latin American bureaucracies. Nevertheless, it is unwarranted to conclude that the extreme forms they take in all of the region's public agencies are merely a consequence of populism and political clientelism. The explosive combination of mounting unemployment, high inflation, and no usable institutions to channel state support to the poor often leaves even the most market-oriented governments with no alternative but to soak up unemployment through public payrolls—or to limit the personnel cuts that are needed to restore some efficiency in public administration. Tragically, the use of public employment to provide temporary respite from social ills erects a barrier to more permanent solutions to these problems.

The collapse of the Latin American state is not only the result of failed economics. It also results from failed politics. Paradoxically, the highly interventionist doctrines that propelled the state to the center of economic and political life and gave it a virtual monopoly over a vast array of activities greatly contributed to its decline. Even while the state was stretched far beyond its own limited capacities, its economic centrality and political voraciousness stifled the emergence and development of spontaneous forms of social organization (clubs, nongovernmental organizations [NGOs], voluntary organizations, civic forums, and so on) that constitute the backbone of what Robert Putnam calls "social capital."[10] Without patterns of social cooperation based on tolerance, trust, and widespread norms of active citizen participation, the modicum of political stability required for the effective operation of public bureaucracies is periodically lost.

In the long term, dismantling its interventionist apparatus will strengthen the state. Focusing on indispensable public tasks, shedding discretionary economic interventions that are a magnet for special interests and corruption, and establishing a more sound fiscal situation should all help to promote the emergence of a more focused and effective public sector. In the short term, however, economic liberalization has eliminated many of the political levers through which the state—especially the executive branch—exercised power and carried out its functions. This has left many countries in the midst of complex transitional instabilities as they seek replacements for old political arrangements and outmoded patterns of political and public action.

Interventionist economic policies furnished central governments with political instruments no longer available under more market-oriented economic regimes. Control over access to low-interest loans, foreign exchange, and private sector permits (to import, export, set prices, invest, divest, and so on) gave the state immense power. Deregulation, privatization, decentralization, and the internationalization of the economy have all diminished the power of the executive branch, and especially that of the president. Under the previous economic and political regimes, the presidency had substantial control and influence over 1) a private sector that depended on the goodwill of the executive to obtain lucrative permits; 2) newspapers and television stations that could not survive without access to government-controlled foreign exchange; 3) labor unions that were either undemocratically repressed or coopted by the party in power; 4) a central bank that, in practice, operated as another department of the government; 5) state and local public administrations that were unilaterally appointed by the executive; and 6) domestic stock markets that were irrelevant. Now all this has changed. Budgetary constraints are extremely rigid, central banks are independent, democratic politics are in full swing, and congress and elected regional authorities constantly assert their autonomy, as do the media and private corporations whose bottom lines no longer depend on the signature of government bureaucrats. Isolationism has been replaced by globalization and regional integration, making trade and investment decisions taken elsewhere a crucial force in determining economic performance and shaping public opinion at home. In the 1990s, the political power and authority of Latin American central governments have greatly diminished. The power, authority, and capacities of governments remain perilously disproportionate to their responsibilities while almost everywhere, expectations and popular frustration with their performance continue to mount.

The Decline of the Latin American State: Statistics, Anecdotes, and Comparisons

Economic bankruptcy. Any discussion of state capacity in Latin America must begin by acknowledging that the region's governments are emerging only now from prolonged economic bankruptcy. Latin American governments remain severely constrained by budgets squeezed dry during the 1980s, when massive spending cuts exacerbated an already poor delivery of public services. Huge expenditures on debt service, money-losing public enterprises, and bloated government ministries converged with a meager level of government tax and tariff collections to produce a crisis that extended well beyond the public sector. Though progress has been made, the region's finances are still precarious, and efforts to rebuild the state face a fearsome challenge from the root causes of Latin America's fiscal demise.

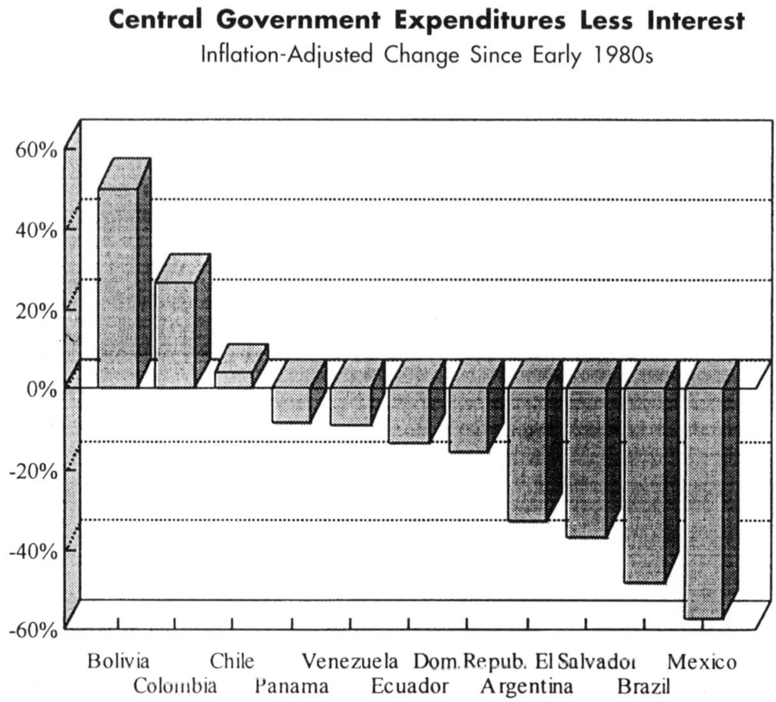

Source: Derived from data presented in IMF, *Government Finance Statistics Yearbook.*

FIGURE 1

The high costs of interest payments, populism, and public enterprises. As is well known, debt service on foreign loans became a crippling drain on Latin American resources during the 1980s. In 1986, for example, Latin American countries paid foreign creditors interest and principal equivalent to 44 percent of the region's exports.[11] Budgets were stripped to make room for debt service, and the state increasingly took on the role of transfer agent, collecting money locally for shipment abroad. This situation improved as international interest rates fell, but it worsened as Latin America's local currencies depreciated. As a share of total spending, interest costs in the region almost doubled—surging from 9 to 17 percent—between 1982 and 1991.[12] The impact on other areas of the public budget was severe. The 1980s saw real, noninterest central government expenditure shrink by one-third in Argentina, and by even larger amounts in other countries. (See Figure 1; details for this and other graphs are presented in the appendix.)

In truth, however, Latin America's dangerous levels of foreign borrowing were more symptom than cause of the region's fiscal demise. Debt and crisis were the natural result of the populist bias that had characterized public spending in most countries. Instead of acting as rule setter and regulator, the state took on the role of reward giver and proprietor. Budget priorities were determined by the strength of designated constituents. State jobs and contracts were important chits in the bidding for political support, so governments extended their control over the productive sectors of Latin American economies. Inefficient nationalized industries required massive borrowing to finance their chronic deficits, but their impact was more than fiscal. While the state was clearly overstretched financially, it had surpassed the limits of its managerial control as well.

The inept collection of taxes and the decline of tariff revenues. The receipts of Latin American tax agencies are dismal. While a few countries' tax administrations have made recent strides toward

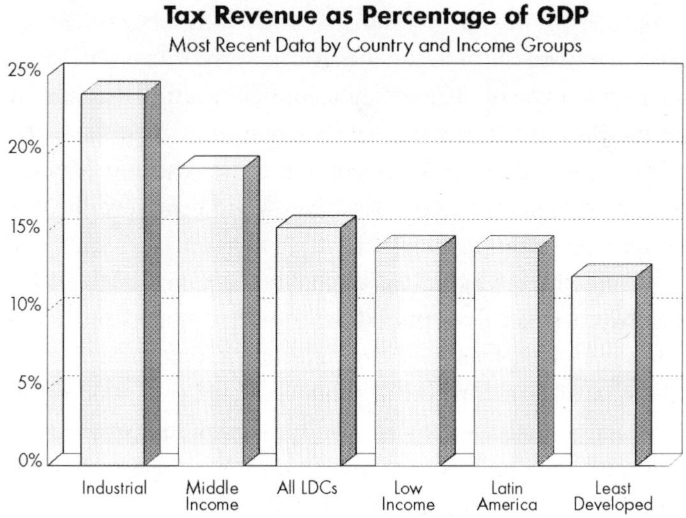

Source: IMF and UNDP, *Human Development Report,* 1993

FIGURE 2

greater capacity in collection, aggregate statistics show that high performers remain the exception. Industrialized countries achieve an average tax collection of 24 percent of GDP, but Latin American collections hover at 14 percent, 1 percentage point below the average for all developing countries, and 5 percentage points below the average for the middle-income group to which most Latin American states belong (see Figure 2).

Examining receipts in more detail, it becomes clear that Latin American tax performance is most dismal in precisely those areas that require the greatest skill and capacity of national tax agencies. Members of the Organization of Economic Cooperation and Development (OECD) tend to raise large portions of their total revenue from personal income taxes: 42 percent in the United States, 39 percent in Japan, 28 percent in the United Kingdom, and 23 percent in Spain. Figures for Latin America are 14 percent in Mexico, 7 percent in Costa Rica, and less than .5 percent in Brazil. These poor results can be blamed largely on administrative incapacity. Prior to Argentina's tax reform, it was estimated that only 17 percent of potential income taxpayers were known to the central tax office, that only 8 percent filed tax returns, and that less than 4 percent actually paid income taxes.[13] In Venezuela, the Office of the Comptroller estimates that only 30 percent of owed income taxes are actually collected.

The ineffectiveness of Latin American governments in collection of personal income taxes has resulted in their overreliance on simpler forms of taxation, most notably on consumption. Excise, sales, and value-added taxes contribute 53 percent of revenue in Mexico and 74 percent of revenue in Peru. Yet taxes levied on specific products tend to skew consumption and often impose costs greater than the revenue raised (though social goals may sometimes justify that welfare loss). More generally applied value-added taxes are less distortionary, but they lack progressivity and their receipts decline rapidly in recession. Concern for both fairness and stability would indicate the use of value-added taxes in conjunction with other taxes, but this is currently beyond the capacity of most Latin American states.

Property taxes are an obvious example of the sort of instrument that should be better utilized. Not only could they diversify national tax bases by generating substantial revenues, but they would also add a greater degree of progressivity to currently regressive systems. Unfortunately, the efficient administration of a property tax is also beyond the capacity of most Latin American states. As a result, even in states where the public sector is considered relatively efficient, property tax receipts are low. In Chile and Costa Rica, for example, they generate revenue equivalent to less than 1 percent of GDP.[14] In Baranquilla, Colombia, revenues are collected on less than 50 percent of the taxable property because only three of the city's ten districts have updated assessment registers.[15]

Widespread trade liberalization means that this dreadful level of tax collection coincides with a rapid decline in revenues from easily administered taxes on trade. In Latin America as a whole, revenue from trade taxes fell from 18 percent of total receipts in 1982 to 11 percent in 1991. Specific countries have had to cope with even larger cuts.[16] Argentina, for example, has seen export-tax revenue fall from 2.2 percent of GDP in 1985 to virtually zero percent of GDP in 1992. Revenue from import taxes has also fallen, despite a boom in imports and improved customs administration.[17] These changes are positive, but they make improvements in other areas of national tax administration nothing less than critical. Such improvements may be underway in Argentina, but most other Latin American countries lag far behind. The state's ability to cope with the region's economic transformation will be in serious doubt as long as national tax bases remain small and revenues poorly collected.

There is no question that the last three to four years have seen a marked improvement in Latin America's fiscal health. Debts have been renegotiated, some loss-making public enterprises have been privatized, cost recovery has improved with price hikes for public services, and a few countries have dramatically improved their tax structures and systems for collection. There is still much to do, however, and fiscal equilibrium remains precarious. Latin American governments will have to keep a watchful eye on their spending at the same time that they must reallocate available funds and find new resources with which to improve their performance.

Operational demise. Latin American states have long been deficient in the delivery of public goods, and the region's fiscal demise has both worsened the condition of its infrastructure and caused a deterioration in the provision of many public services.

Infrastructure and maintenance. Maintenance is both the least glamorous and one of the most important of government functions. Examining the infrastructure and maintenance expenditures of Latin American countries during the 1980s shows that the region has substantial catching up to do. Since the early 1980s, real spending on new infrastructure has fallen in 11 of 13 studied countries (see Figure 3).

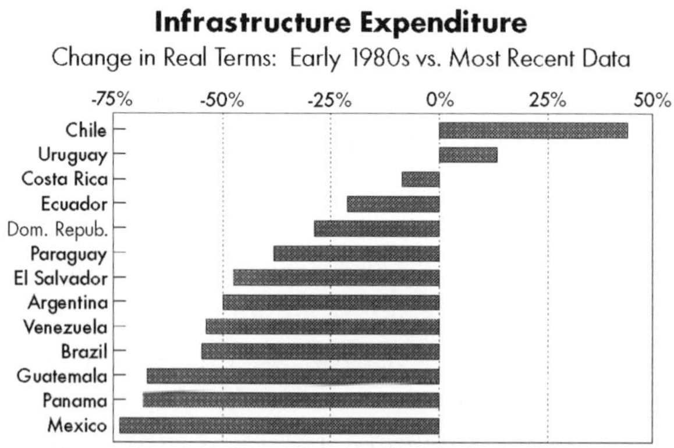

Source: IMF, *Government Finance Statistics Yearbook,* 1992

FIGURE 3

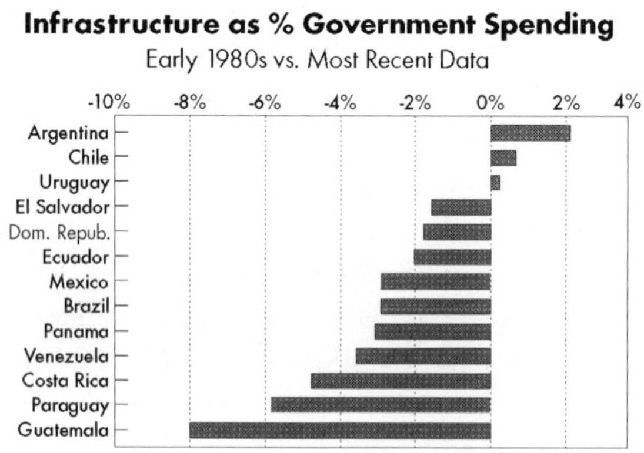

Source: IMF, *Government Finance Statistics Yearbook,* 1992

FIGURE 4

All but three countries have seen infrastructure expenditure fall as a percentage of total government spending (see Figure 4).

Investment budgets can perhaps be expected to suffer during fiscal crises, but Latin American governments have also slashed their current expenditures in ways that may return to haunt them. Real spending on infrastructural maintenance has fallen in over two-thirds of the studied countries. The results can be devastating, completely wiping out the "savings" achieved by budget cutbacks. Ecuador, for example, has lost over 5 percent of its paved-road network since 1987 because of inadequate maintenance. Reconstructing the lost routes will cost 175 times the amount that would have been required to maintain them adequately.[18]

Other public goods. States are generally considered responsible for other elements of infrastructure as well, regardless of whether government or a private agent is the actual provider. Systems that supply safe water, health care, and education are commonly expected. How does Latin America measure up?

Rural areas are always more difficult to serve, and Latin America's performance reflects this. Only 56 percent of rural Latin Americans have access to safe drinking water, a standard considerably below

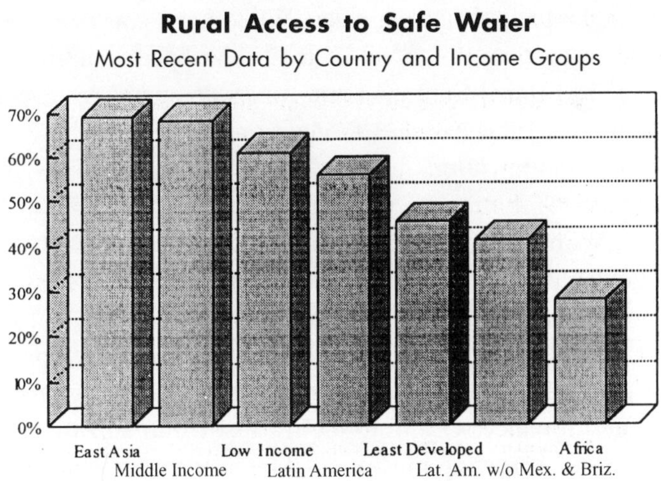

Source: WHO and UNDP, *Human Development Report,* 1993. East Asia excludes China.

FIGURE 5

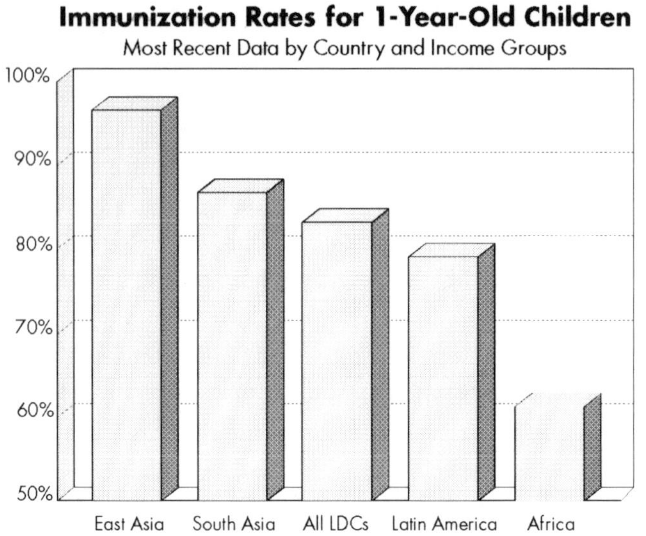

Source: WHO, UNICEF, and UNDP, *Human Development Report,* 1993

FIGURE 6

that of the East Asian countries that many Latin American states would like to emulate as well as the middle-income aggregate to which most Latin American countries belong (see Figure 5). On average, even low-income developing countries have access rates 5 percentage points higher than the Latin American mean. While Latin America as a whole performed better than the group of least developed countries, removing Mexico and Brazil from the Latin American aggregate reverses that result, with only rural Africans faring worse.

Using immunization rates as an indicator of access to basic medical services, Latin America trails all regions except Africa (see Figure 6). With an immunization rate of 79 percent, Latin America lags behind East Asia by a full 18 percentage points. South Asian access to immunization is 7 percentage points higher than in Latin America, and Latin America falls below the average developing country by 4 percentage points. Mexico and Brazil do little to pull up their region's performance. Omitting them causes immunization rates to drop only 1 point, leaving most Latin American children about 19 percent less likely to be immunized than East Asian children—and 5 percent less likely than the average developing-country child.

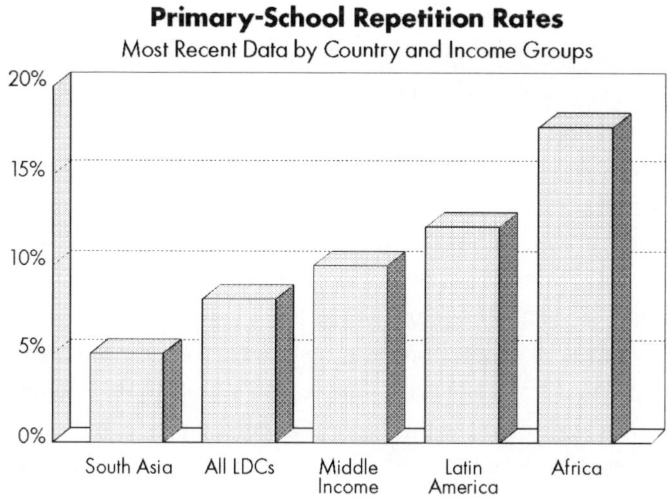

Source: UNESCO and UNDP, *Human Development Report,* 1993

FIGURE 7

Governmental performance in education is equally poor. Unfortunately, Latin American primary-school students are 50 percent more likely than the average developing-country child to repeat a grade. They are more than twice as likely to do so as the average South Asian child (see Figure 7).

The point of these comparisons is both to show how poorly the Latin American state has done and to demonstrate how much better it can and must perform. It would be tragic to interpret the lessons of the 1980s simplistically. Minimizing the state's role is a must in the productive sectors, but revitalizing it in other areas is equally important.

A major development of the 1980s was Latin America's recognition that many "public" goods can be produced and delivered more efficiently by private agents. Privately built roads, for example, partly explain the decline in public infrastructure expenditure seen in Mexico. Most states, however, have yet to turn to private providers of infrastructure on that scale. If and when they do, government officials must be able to ensure their satisfactory performance. Yet public agencies and regulators are at risk of being outnegotiated by private contractors. Improving the efficiency of public agencies will be costly, but it will be money well spent; the success of a market-driven strategy rests on the ability of government to ensure the smooth delivery of infrastructure and other public goods from myriad sources. It would be helpful if market observers learned to distinguish between "good" and "bad" government expenditure.

Perhaps the region's periodic bank failures will strike closer to home. After all, improved prudential supervision—a public good—can prevent (or at least minimize) the chaos that follows a bank's collapse. Unfortunately, supervision is lacking in most Latin American countries. Supervisory agencies frequently lack the legal or practical authority to assume control of institutions edging toward failure; bank examiners are underskilled and underpaid. The region's high reserve requirements are in part a substitute for this lack of adequate prudential supervision, but the costs of this strategy are high. Consumers and businesses must pay for tighter credit, with little added security. High reserve requirements alone have been unable to keep banks from going under.

Organizational collapse. The Latin American state suffers as much from organizational problems as it does from fiscal ones. Not only are most governments locked into employing large numbers of unnecessary workers, they can offer only the most inadequate compensation to the managerial staff by whose efforts state success will be determined. Turnover of top officials is high, and the process of decentralization is having short-term negative effects on the delivery of public services.

Wage burdens. At least rhetorically, state downsizing has been government gospel throughout most of Latin America since the mid-1980s. But while cash-strapped governments have shed numerous functions and enterprises, few public employees have actually lost jobs. Outside of Chile and Argentina, most state payrolls have remained steady or even grown (see Box 2).

If this seems a victory for public workers, it is a Pyrrhic one at best. Although civil-service layoffs were too politically costly to bear, the fiscal imperative confronting governments did not disappear. Since the numbers of public workers could not be reduced, wages were squeezed instead. Public-wage losses far exceeded salary cuts in other sectors. As shown in Box 2, Latin America's real

Box 2
Wages of Sin: The Collapse of Government Salaries in Latin America

Latin American governments kept their employees . . .
Employment by Sector

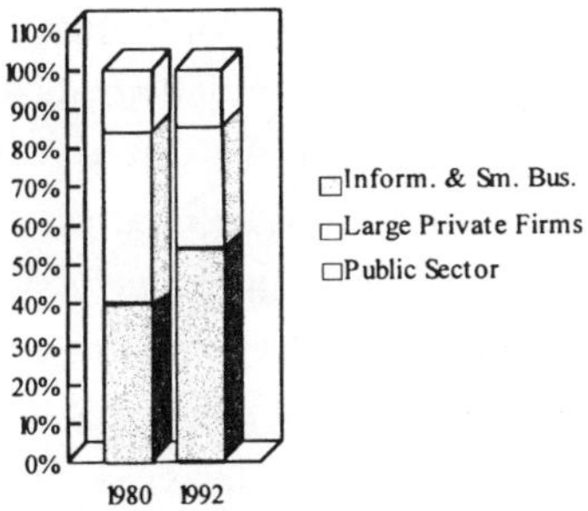

Source: ILO, PREALC

Of all formal-sector workers, public employees suffered the steepest cuts in real wages during the 1980s. State wage increases were held well below the pace of inflation, and real salaries were cut by 30 percent over the course of the decade, more than triple the drop experienced in private enterprise. Only those employed in the informal sector were less able to protect their real earnings. But cutting pay without cutting payrolls was insufficient to relieve the heavy burden imposed by public-sector wages. State salaries still consume a much greater portion of government revenue in Latin America than they do in either OECD or other middle-income economies.

But paid them less . . .
Real Latin American Wages by Sector

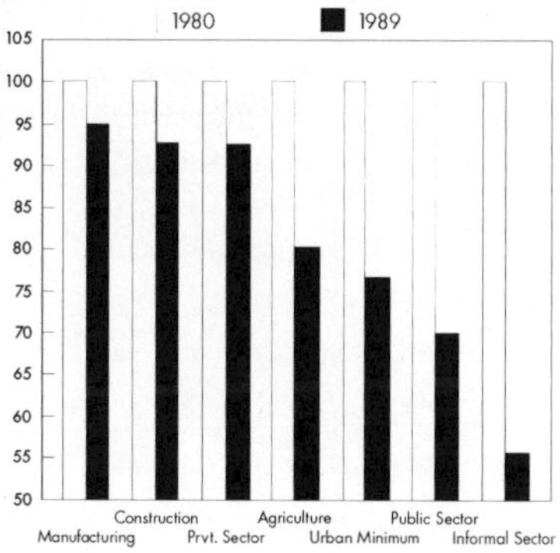

Source: ILO, PREALC.

And saved little.
Public Wages as Percentage of Tax Revenue

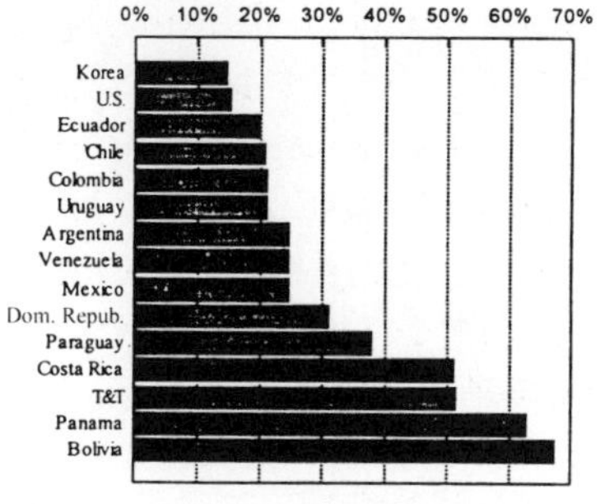

Source: IMF, *GFS Yearbook 1992.*

public-sector wages fell 30 percent between 1980 and 1989, more than triple the drop experienced in private enterprise. Some countries' civil servants fared even worse. The purchasing power of Argentina's public wages fell by nearly two-thirds between 1980 and 1992, as compared with the 25-percent loss suffered by the country's construction and industrial workers (see Figure 8). The real monthly wage for economists in Brazil's ministry of planning during 1992 was one-fifth the level of the same salary in March of 1985.[19]

Despite the pain it has caused, the strategy of maintaining employee numbers while cutting real wages has failed in its fiscal purpose. Salaries can be cut only so far, and the savings have proved insufficient to relieve Latin America's high public-wage burden. The third chart in Box 2 makes the point clearly. Wages consume 37 percent of tax revenue in Paraguay, 51 percent in Costa Rica, and an enormous 67 percent in Bolivia. In contrast, Korea spends only 14 percent of tax revenue on public salaries. Ecuador's results, the lowest in Latin America at 19.4 percent, are interesting in that the Ecuadoran government relied solely on wage reductions to meet its fiscal challenge and thus epitomized the regional pattern. After adjusting for inflation, the country's expenditure on

Purchasing Power of Argentine Wages

Variations by Sector, 1984–92

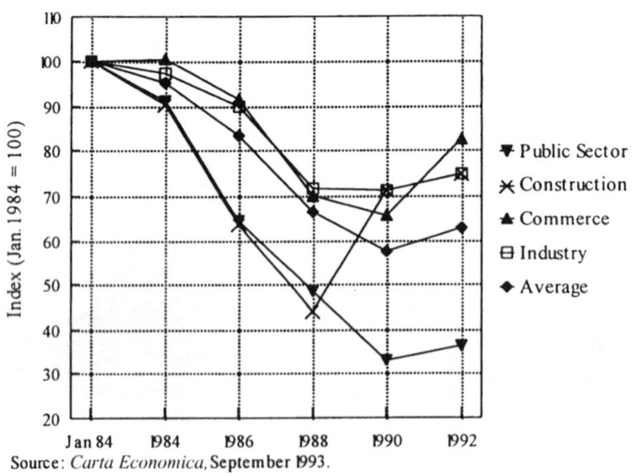

Source: *Carta Economica*, September 1993.

FIGURE 8

public wages grew by only 3.5 percent between 1981 and 1990, despite a 59 percent increase in the number of state employees.

It is clear, however, that Latin America's wage reductions are a short-term fix and have delayed the opportunity to free up much greater resources through a rational assessment of the state's personnel needs. The damage is more than fiscal. Deep wage cuts may be less humane than the layoffs they are meant to prevent, and such cuts frequently cause the quality of government services to decline. Peruvian teachers lost 75 percent of their real wages between 1980 and 1989, causing trained instructors to flee the field for less hard-hit sectors. As a result, the proportion of uncertified teachers doubled to 50 percent by 1990.[20] This may be a factor in Peruvian children's extremely high repetition rates.

Salary structure. While Latin America's public wages have fallen across the board, top managers lose the most when they choose a career in government service. The gap between public and private compensation for similar functions grows with seniority, creating an inverse relationship between responsibility and relative wages. This structure works directly against recent efforts to create a lean and highly skilled civil service; the appeal of a public wage increases dramatically as skill levels decline.

The salaries confronting ministers in particular are detailed in Box 3. An increase is clearly indicated for most countries. Ministerial wages in most Latin American governments hover between $10,000 and $30,000 annually. Venezuela pays its ministers only $13,000. Fast-growing Asian and African countries are more generous. Taiwan's ministers earn close to $70,000, and ministers in Botswana are paid $32,000 per year *before* cash allowances allocated by the president.

Turnover. Since 1988, the average minister in Latin America has held on to his job for less than 15 months (see Box 4). Worse, the average is that high only because of relatively long tenures in Mexico and, to a much lesser extent, Colombia and Chile. Excluding those three countries causes Latin America's average ministerial tenure to drop below 12 months. Argentina and Brazil changed

Box 3
"If You Pay Peanuts, You'll Get Monkeys for Your Ministers"

Latin American ministers are poorly paid . . .
Annual Minister Salaries in 1994
U.S. Dollars

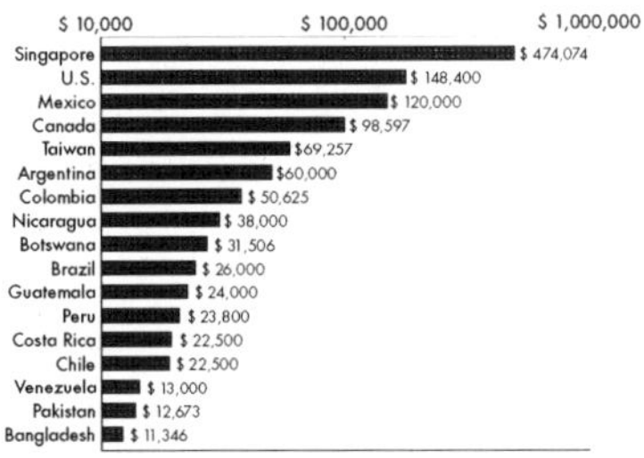

Collected by the author from official sources.
Known cash bonuses included.

This was the argument used by Singapore's Prime Minister Goh Chok Tong when he tried to stop his ministers' flight to the private sector by raising their wages to US$474,000 per year.[1]

Salaries for Latin American ministers pale in comparison. (The graph at left had to be drawn with a logarithmic scale just so they could be seen.) While Mexican ministers have recently received a large raise, the numbers drop quickly from there. Ministers in Chile, Costa Rica, Peru, Guatemala, and Brazil earn under $30,000 apiece. Venezuela brings up the rear with salaries of only $13,000, little better than those in Bangladesh. Salaries for directors and others below the ministerial level tend to be much lower, so it is no surprise that other Latin American public salaries are a small fraction of what is available in the private sector.

More interesting is that, relative to the private sector, receptionists in Latin America's public bureaucracies are better paid than the managers they work for. In Uruguay, for example, a public administrative worker receives 90 percent of a private-sector receptionist's salary, while government division directors earn only 38 percent of a private managerial salary.

Public enterprises generally pay better than the central government, but the gap relative to the private sector remains large. In 1993, top managers in Venezuela's public enterprises earned only 35 percent of the wages of their private-sector counterparts.[2]

These salaries are consistent with the notion that Latin American public officials frequently see their postings as occasional diversifications of other careers that will become more lucrative following their brief stints in high public office. The opportunity for quick gains through corruption are also clearly a motivator for some.

And public wages fall with seniority.
Public Wage as Percentage of
Comparable Private Wage

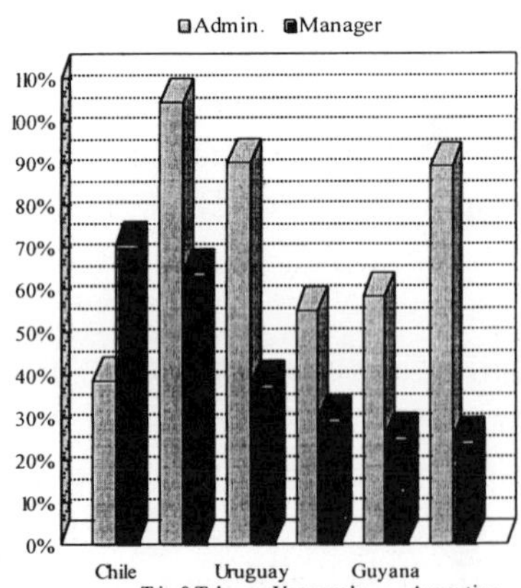

Source: Gary Reid, World Bank, 1993.

[1]*Financial Times,* 8 December 1993.
[2]Private communication, HAY Consulting Group.

Box 4
Here Today, Gone Tomorrow: Latin America's Ministerial Turnover

Latin American Ministers face short tenures . . .
A Minister's Months in Office

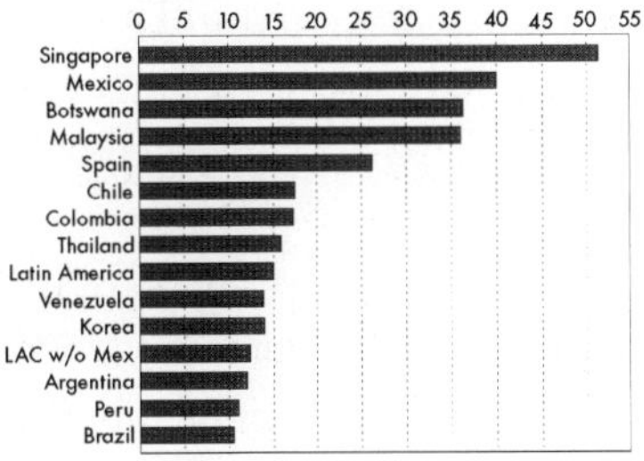

Whether they manage an economic . . .
Economic Portfolios: Number of Ministers, 1988–93

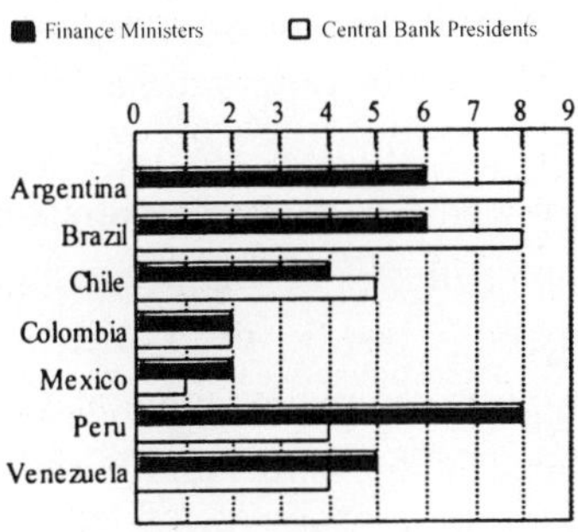

Or a social portfolio.
Social Portfolios: Number of Ministers, 1988–93

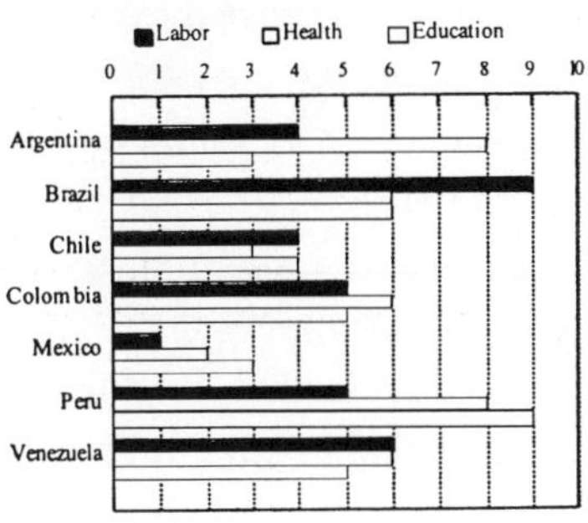

Ministers in Latin American governments serve an average of only 14.6 months in office. When countries with the longest ministerial tenures (Mexico, Chile, and Colombia) are excluded, the regional average falls to just over 11.5 months. This instability casts serious doubt on governments' capacities to implement and manage the fundamental changes called for by the region's economic transformation.

Economic portfolios fared little better than socially oriented ministries. Excluding the top three performers, Latin American ministers of labor, health, and education served an average of 11.5 months. Ministers of finance and central bank presidents held on to their jobs only six days longer, and Argentina and Brazil went through a central bank president every nine months. Such frequent turnover would seem a major hurdle for countries eager to demonstrate their stability to world financial markets.

Americans frequently bemoan the inefficiencies of the presidential transition that occurs every four years in their country. It should be remembered that a "mini-transition" must be endured each time a new minister comes to power in Latin America. The government and the ministry in question must absorb not just a new leader, but also a fresh group of sub-ministerial directors, advisors, and others.

Moreover, the amount of time required to assemble this team can only grow as tenures are shortened and job security is decreased. Ministers are understandably hard-pressed to recruit top aides when the life expectancy for their positions is only a few months.

Source: Based on data presented in *Chiefs of State and Cabinet Members of Foreign Governments.* See appendix for full details.

their central-bank governors an average of once every nine months. All of these figures compare poorly with those seen in most countries outside the region. Spanish ministers averaged 26 months in office during the same period, while ministers in Botswana and Malaysia served an average of three years each.

Box 3 addresses ministerial salaries. It is worth noting that the highest-paid ministers (found in Singapore) also tend to remain in office the longest. Pay is not everything, of course, and inflating salaries will not necessarily compensate for failed policies. Clearly, however, a radical improvement in government performance cannot be achieved when leadership is so fleeting. Peru has one of the world's highest primary-school repetition rates; the average student is in the first grade for 1.6 years. What meaningful improvement can be made by a minister of education who is in office for only eight months?

This instability in high positions is one of Latin America's fundamental problems, but there is a surprising lack of data that could be used to analyze turnover rates for correlations with inflation, economic cycles, and other phenomena. Such relationships are important, but available information restricts one to anecdotal observations that are nonetheless time-consuming to construct. During the six-year interval for which data were studied for this paper, for example, Venezuelan ministers served an average of 13.8 months in office. One might assume that this relatively high rate of turnover is due to the political and economic upheavals of the period. In fact, more fundamental factors are at work. The average tenure of Venezuela's ministers of industry from 1856 to the present is only nine months.

Decentralization. Sweeping decentralization has accompanied Latin America's movement toward democracy. Direct mayoral elections have replaced central government appointments for the first time in Colombia, Paraguay, and Venezuela, while municipal elections have recently been held in Chile and Bolivia after suspensions of 19 and 35 years, respectively.[21] Perhaps more important, by 1990, Latin America's 14,000 municipalities had effectively doubled their share of total public spending from the levels that predominated only eight years before (see Figure 9). This transfer of political, economic, and administrative authority to local governments is a

Spending by Municipalities

Share of Total Public Spending in Latin America

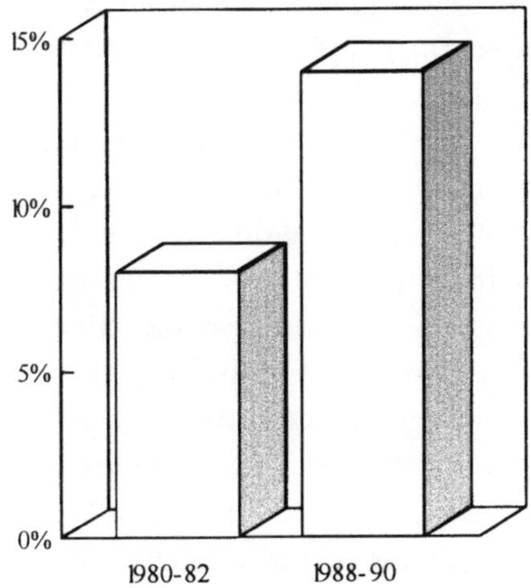

Source: *Oxford Analytica*, 1994.

FIGURE 9

positive development, and was necessary to counteract the over-centralization that had previously developed under authoritarian regimes. Numerous public services are simply better performed at the local level, where accountability is leveraged by the proximity of end-users. Local schools, for example, increasingly respond to those they serve, rather than to an ill-fitting model designed for the convenience of distant bureaucrats.

That being so, why include decentralization in a list of factors contributing to the organizational problems of the state? The reason is that the early stages of decentralization are inevitably plagued by underperformance and financial disarray. While Latin America's bureaucracies have fared poorly in the capital, they have suffered even more in the provinces. Both institutionally and organizationally, local governments are weak and often unable to fulfill their new responsibilities. The water authority in Guatemala City, for example, is unable to account for 70 percent of the water in its system, much less recover the relevant costs from those who are using it.[22] Local administrations have been somewhat more adept at securing central government revenues. Though both the national and local governments would be better off with a systematic division of total public resources, in the absence of such a system, individual local governments opt to maximize their own receipts, to the detriment of the whole.

The problem is rooted in the central government's weak coordinating capacity, and the failure to connect revenues with responsibility. The common result is the distribution of sizeable revenues to the provinces without a compensatory contribution to the costs of government services. The reverse has also occurred—some regional governments have been transferred massive responsibilities without the resources or authority required to execute them. Twin challenges are raised by either situation. The managerial capacity of the provinces must be built at the same time that the coordinating capacity of the center is increased.

The devolution of power is a complex process, but Latin America's decentralizations have tended to be explained by charts and promulgated by decrees. Such reforms are truncated, for they fail to confront the revenue-responsibility trade-off and the massive capacity building required to make decentralization a success.

What to Do? Where to Begin?

The next stage of reforms in Latin America is different not only in that it will require more coalition building, political maneuvering, and managerial capacity than did the initial, stabilization-oriented, decree-driven stage. It is also different in that, in contrast to some of the ideas that guided the actions of presidents and their cabinets during Stage I, the theoretical underpinnings of Stage II reforms are still primitive and unrefined. Once presidents and cabinets developed the political will to launch Stage I reforms, they could rely on a set of widely accepted theories that offered precise policy prescriptions for stabilizing the economy, for example.

Most Stage II reforms lack firm guidelines. Just compare the theoretical support available to a government that has decided to correct the distortions of the exchange rate to available guidelines for reforming the administration of justice. Reforming the trade regime may be difficult, cumbersome, and politically costly, but trade theory at least provides a coherent and robust set of targets, tools, and principles to orient government actions in this area. Civil-service reform is as cumbersome and politically costly. But public administration and management techniques do not provide a reliable set of prescriptions to help governments make sense of their policy options and their consequences. Of course, career planning, a merit system, regular training, and adequate compensation should be obvious goals of any civil-service reform. Unfortunately, experience in developing countries shows that, more often than not, the adoption of such lofty goals results in an even more unresponsive, costly, and inefficient public bureaucracy. This is because the successful implementation of such reforms requires preconditions that are either not well understood or hard to induce. For example, paying more competitive salaries in the public sector is probably indispensable. Doing so without ensuring that recruitment and promotion are based more on merit than on political connections only serves to increase the price paid by society for the same inefficient and corrupt public bureaucracy. To make career planning a positive tool for a public agency, it is necessary that the organization not be subject to the constant radical swings in its priorities, budgets, and staffing requirements that are so typical of public-sector agencies in Latin America.

While there may be a consensus about the main traits that characterize a civil service suited to the needs and constraints of a developing country, there is only confusion about the specific actions governments should take to promote the emergence of such traits. Who could dispute the urgent need to lower the vulnerability of Latin American courts to capture by narrow political and economic interests? Who could argue against a decreased level of turnover of top personnel? The problem is how to bring about these desirable outcomes.

Institutional weakness and the low effectiveness of the public administration have long been recognized as a major constraint on the progress of less developed countries. In recent years, however, that reality has been blurred by a fascination with the relative simplicity, intellectual elegance, and rapid results of macroeconomic management, along with an aversion to state-centered solutions. Economic liberalization, privatization, decentralization, and the general shrinkage of the state did reduce the impossibly heavy burdens that previous economic schemes imposed on a weak public administration. But the illusion that rapid progress could be maintained without first overcoming the institutional hurdles that had historically blocked development led to an underestimation of the urgency with which more efficient public management is needed.

Progress in this area requires first and foremost that practitioners and researchers alike recognize state capacity as the central precondition of development. The same intellectual attention, political priority, and resources given in the 1980s to finding cures to the problems caused by high indebtedness, macroeconomic disarray, and excessive state intervention should now be dedicated to finding ways to alleviate the consequences of institutional decay and the withering of the state.

No silver bullet is likely to be found. It will not be possible to endow swiftly the public sector with capacities that it never had, or to restore quickly some of the faculties lost to years of institutional erosion. The process is bound to be long, cumbersome, and confusing. It is, therefore, critical to start now and to concentrate talent and resources on the development of a proven methodology for this task. While no comprehensive and proven road map is currently available for governments committed to putting institutional development at the top of their agenda, it is clear that success in this endeavor will critically depend on their ability to move effectively on three major fronts: money, organization, and politics.

Money: From budget cuts to budget redeployment. The Latin American state desperately needs to increase spending and investment both on its internal operations and on the provision of indispensable public goods and services that will not or cannot be provided by the private sector. These are currently in gross undersupply throughout the region. Water, infrastructure, police, education, and justice are only a few examples.

Nonetheless, institution building and increasing state capacities cannot become excuses for lax fiscal and monetary policies, for the inefficient expansion of the public bureaucracy, or for permissive labor practices in the public sector. Stage II reforms must be implemented while maintaining and deepening those implemented in Stage I. Institution building in the midst of high inflation and other ills remedied by Stage I reforms would likely be impossible. On the other hand, enhancing state capacities does add to the fiscal strains that continue to challenge Latin American governments.

In some countries, it may be possible to increase government revenues to satisfy its needs. In the great majority of cases, however, moving to a sustainable fiscal situation will also require cutting public spending and investment in some activities and regions and reassigning the freed-up resources to new priorities. Governments will be forced to confront the politics of budget redeployment, which differ markedly from the politics of general fiscal austerity characteristic of Stage I. The politics of reducing all budgets by 10 percent are quite different from the politics of taking 10 percent from one ministry and giving it to another.

Privatization and improved tax collection contributed to the swift move toward fiscal stability recently exhibited by most Latin American countries. But public deficits were reduced mainly through massive budget cuts that affected all sectors, regions, and activities. In the future, public funds to fight poverty and deliver social services will have to come from the budgets of the military or other sectors that have traditionally enjoyed easy access to public coffers. In most of Latin America, for example, universities consume the lion's share of the education budget. Rather than relying on new fiscal revenues, increased funds for vocational and primary education will more likely have to come from the lopsided budgets that rioting university students once extorted from permissive ministers.

In sum, building public institutions requires money, but those funds should not be obtained at the expense of fiscal stability. Instead, public spending and investment must be restructured in ways that imply a profound redesign of the state's operations and budget. Without this redesign of the state, the fiscal achievements of recent years will become increasingly hard to sustain. Democracy will also be subject to strong destabilizing pressures unless enough funding to upgrade state performance can be secured.

Organization: The paradox of the forgotten price. "Getting prices right" was the leitmotif that guided many Stage I economic reforms. From eggs to the exchange rate and from electricity to interest rates, the goal was to minimize the gap between prices decided by governments and those defined by markets. In many countries, this gap became so large that hoarding, black market speculation, and chronic shortages made government policies unsustainable and paved the way for the market reforms that ensued. Price corrections were painful and exacted a heavy toll from society, particularly from the poor. But once the corrections were made, the flexibility of prices stimulated investment and eliminated many of the socially regressive consequences of price controls. Paradoxically, in the wave of efforts to "get prices right," a price that was usually forgotten and left to lag behind at artificially low levels was the price paid for the work of the public managers in charge of getting all other prices "right."

In almost all countries, public salaries trail those in the private sector, especially at the highest levels. In Latin America the disparity between public and private salaries has always been especially pronounced. In recent years, market reforms and fiscal austerity widened this gap dangerously. The liberalization of markets created strong incentives for the development of the private sector, thus boosting both demand and salaries for competent managers. At the same time, fiscal austerity drastically repressed salaries in the public sector, further increasing their distance from the salaries paid to private-sector managers. In the future, governments will have to pay as much attention to these prices as they do to the exchange rate. A distorted and unrealistic salary structure in the public sector is as damaging and unsustainable in the long run as an artificially low rate of interest.

The paradox of the forgotten price is a metaphor for the many other forgotten reforms needed to upgrade the organization of the public sector. The state apparatus not only needs to alter radically its organizational structure, it also needs to overhaul and modernize its organizational processes. Policy planning, budgeting, personnel practices, information systems, coordination mechanisms, control and oversight, maintenance, and general services are realms that have obviously been deeply affected by decades of neglect, improvisation, politicization, and lack of resources, especially skilled and stable personnel. It is hard to find a Latin American government official who disagrees with the statement that the state's performance in carrying out these functions is dismal and that such tasks must receive a greater share of attention and resources. It is even harder to find governments that actually address these issues in a systematic and effective way. The inner workings of public bureaucracies should receive as much attention from the highest levels of government as threats from macroeconomic instability received in the recent past.

Improving public organizations requires simultaneous actions on many fronts. While no agreement exists about the optimal sequence that reforms aimed in this direction should follow, one important condition without which the organizational efficiency of the state will be difficult to improve is the reform of labor laws and practices. Labor reform is still pending in most of Latin America.[23] The region's labor markets are almost uniformly distorted by a legacy of misguided labor laws that seriously undermine the possibility of restructuring the public sector in general and the social-sector agencies in particular. These agencies tend to be the largest employers in the country and are, therefore, the most affected by labor regulations that increase the costs, conflicts and implementation time associated with any change in the institutional status quo. Creating an environment in which organizational efficiency can emerge in the public sector should be the first order of business for governments.

Politics: Freeing space for bureaucratic excellence. In the same way that macroeconomic instability hinders institution-building efforts, political instability has nefarious effects on governmental performance and greatly inhibits positive organizational change. It is, in fact, quite naive to worry about organizational development in the public sector when the instability of the political environment in which public agencies have to operate makes for volatile public policies and ephemeral management teams. Agencies that are captured by private interests, labor unions, or political bosses not even part of the government, are also unavoidably plagued by organizational conditions that hinder the emergence of sound managerial practices.

Nonetheless, in some countries, a political consensus has often emerged regarding the need to avoid the politicization of the staffing and functioning of specific public bodies. Such consensus is often maintained for long periods and, in some cases, has even survived episodes of political commotion and bitter partisan confrontations. Public bodies in charge of managing the principal export sectors, for example, are often treated with great care by politicians and are usually given significant autonomy in their staffing and promotion decisions. In general, these agencies enjoy a higher level of political insulation than do other public organizations in their country. That is the case, for example, with CODELCO, Chile's state-owned copper company; national oil companies such as Petroleos de Venezuela, PETROBRAS, and ECOPETROL; Colombia's Fondo del Cafe; and some of Central America's agencies that oversee banana exports. In recent years, several countries in Latin America have granted legal autonomy to their central banks, thus shielding them even further not only from partisan politics but also from the influence of the administration. The relatively new "social emergency funds" in Chile, Bolivia, Peru, and Guatemala have exhibited a high level of technical competence and have successfully avoided the ills that, in those same countries, plague all other institutions in charge of assisting the poor.

This sets an intriguing precedent. When an objective or an organization becomes sufficiently important in the eyes of the main political actors, implicit or explicit pacts are often reached to safeguard it against undue political interference and provide it with sufficient resources. By its very nature, this tactic cannot be generalized to the entire public sector. But governments and political leaders of different sectors should increasingly recognize the need to agree to protect crucial public agencies from the ravages of partisan politics and political clientelism. The public agencies targeted for this treatment will probably vary from country to country.

The elimination—or even a significant reduction—of the weight that narrow political calculations have in the functioning of a public agency, together with the commitment to endow the agency with the financial and material resources that it needs to operate effectively and attract competent personnel, can certainly set the stage for important gains in productivity and efficiency. On the other hand, precautions should be taken to avoid the natural propensity for the shields against undue political interference eventually to become barriers against the proper accountability and public control under which all state organizations must operate.

Evidently, this approach to public-sector reform is neither as all-encompassing nor as swift as the macroeconomic shocks that induced the impressive economic turnarounds of the early 1990s. For most of the region's population, however, seeing at least some of their public institutions become more efficient and reliable would be a welcome surprise. In fact, a working public agency would be more of a "positive shock" than the very impressive but always abstract macroeconomic indicators of which governments are fond of boasting.

Reaching that goal will require governments to find a new base on which to build their mandates. The fear of impending economic debacle must be replaced by a widely held consensus about the best route to progress. Achieving such consensus will not be easy. But while the politics of consensus are more challenging than the politics of fear, they are also more lasting.

Appendix

Fiscal, wage, and infrastructure data. Most fiscal, wage, and infrastructure data presented in this paper were drawn from the International Monetary Fund's *Government Finance Statistics Yearbook,* 1992. Real figures were adjusted by the GDP deflator, and a full spreadsheet is available upon request. Because of reporting delays in various countries, slightly different beginning and ending years were used in such comparisons as "change during the 1980s."

In general, data were analyzed for the following periods: Argentina, 1982–89; Bolivia, 1984–91; Brazil, 1982–90; Chile, 1981–88; Colombia, 1981–89; Costa Rica, 1982–91; Dominican Republic, 1981–90; Ecuador, 1981–90; El Salvador, 1982–90; Guatemala, 1981–89; Mexico, 1982–90; Panama, 1981–90; Paraguay, 1981–90; Peru, 1982–91; Uruguay, 1981–90; Venezuela, 1982–91; United States, 1983–91; Korea, 1983–91. In some cases, however, wage or infrastructural expenditure data were available only for shorter intervals.

As has been the practice in previous studies, government expenditures on "transportation and communication" were used as a proxy for infrastructure, while expenditures on "nonwage goods and services" were used as a proxy for infrastructural maintenance. Bolivian expenditures on infrastructure were studied but not included owing to unavailability of pre-1986 data.

Social data. Most social data were drawn from the referenced United Nations agencies and reflect the most recent available figures for each country.

Ministerial turnover rates. The names of all ministers of finance, education, labor, and health, as well as central bank presidents serving between 1988 and 1993, were taken from the past six years of the U.S. Government periodical *Chiefs of State and Cabinet Members of Foreign Governments.* (A full spreadsheet with turnover rates by ministry, country, region, and type of portfolio is available upon request.) Turnover rates were then calculated on the simplifying assumption that the first minister to appear in the publication began service on 1 January 1988. This allowed a comparison of the numbers of ministers to hold a given portfolio across the same period of time in different countries. Average turnover rates, however, may be exaggerated by that assumption if, for example, the minister serving in January 1988 had already been in office for a long time. This problem was unavoidable if a uniform period was to be studied for all countries. Countries studied were Argentina, Brazil, Chile, Colombia, Mexico, Peru, Venezuela, Spain, Korea, Malaysia, Singapore, Thailand, and Botswana.

NOTES

1. Inflation was 19 percent if Brazil's rate of 2,000 percent is excluded from the Latin American aggregate. Inflation was 410 percent if Brazil is included.

2. See Larry Diamond, "Democracy in Latin America: Degrees, Illusions and Directions for Consolidation" in Tom Farer, ed., *Reconstructing Sovereignty in a Democratic Age* (Washington, D.C.: Inter-American Dialogue, 1994); and Jorge Domínguez and Abraham Lowenthal, "The Challenges of Democratic Governance in Latin America and the Caribbean: Sounding an Alarm" (paper presented at the Ninth Plenary Meeting of the Inter-American Dialogue, Washington, D.C., April 1994.

3. See Stephan Haggard and Robert R. Kaufman, "The State in the Initiation and Consolidation of Market Oriented Reform" in Louis Putterman and Dietrich Rueschemeyer, eds., *State and Market in Development: Synergy or Rivalry?* (Boulder, Colo.: Lynne Rienner Publishers, 1992); and Moisés Naím, *Paper Tigers and Minotaurs: The Politics of Venezuela's Economic Reforms* (Washington, D.C.: Carnegie Endowment for International Peace, 1993).

4. Many argue that this is a recurrent characteristic in the launching of neoliberal reforms everywhere. See, for example, Adam Przeworski and Susan Stokes, "Political Dynamics of Economic Reforms: Six Facts in Search of an Explanation" (paper presented at a conference on "Political Dynamics of Economic Reforms," University of Chicago, May 1993).

5. See Terry Lynn Karl and Philippe C. Schmitter, "Modes of Transitions and Types of Democracy in Latin America, Southern and Eastern Europe," *International Social Science Journal* 128 (May 1991); and Guillermo O'Donnell, "Delegative Democracy," *Journal of Democracy* 5 (January 1994): 55–69.

6. There has been much debate and analysis of the optimal sequencing of the different reforms (prices, fiscal adjustment, the exchange-rate regime, trade, finance, agriculture, privatization, labor, social policies, etc.) and of their pace (shock versus gradualism). In principle, a clear differentiation has become common between measures aimed at restoring macroeconomic equilibrium (stabilization) and those designed to alter the boundaries between the private and public sectors and the way in which the different sectors of the economy are structured and operate. There is a consensus that most other changes will be harder, impossible, or short-lived if macroeconomic disarray is prevalent, and that it is therefore

necessary to concentrate all efforts on economic stabilization before anything else. While the two broad categories of reform are usually labeled "Macroeconomic Stabilization" and "Structural Reform," this paper refers to "Stage I" and "Stage II" reforms, for in fact, stabilization and structural change occur in both stages of the reform process.

7. Stephen Haggard and Robert R. Kaufman, *The Political Economy of Democratic Transitions* (Princeton: Princeton University Press, forthcoming).

8. Peter Evans, "Rethinking Embedded Autonomy" (Unpublished manuscript, University of California, Berkeley, September 1993), 2, 10.

9. Carmelo Mesa Lago, *Social Security in Latin America* (Washington, D.C.: Inter-American Development Bank, 1991).

10. Robert Putnam, *Making Democracy Work: Civic Traditions in Modern Italy* (Princeton: Princeton University Press, 1993). In fact, as noted above, it is becoming increasingly clear that the only hope for more effective state action in Latin America lies in the decentralization of political and administrative decision making. The active involvement and widespread participation of local communities are indispensable if the problems that are currently plaguing this process are to be minimized.

11. World Bank, *World Debt Tables, 1993–1994,* (Washington, D.C. The World Bank, 1994), 186.

12. Oxford Analytica, Ltd., *The Role of the Public Sector in Latin America in the 1990s and Beyond: A Study Prepared for the Inter-American Development Bank* (Washington, D.C. IDB, 1994), 10.

13. Viviana Durán, "Una estimación de la función de recaudación del IVA" (Unpublished manuscript, Buenos Aires, 1989). Cited in World Bank, *Argentina: Tax Policy for Stabilization and Economic Recovery,* Country Study Series (Washington, D.C.: World Bank, 1990).

14. International Monetary Fund, *Government Finance Statistics Yearbook,* (Washington, D.C.: International Monetary Fund, 1992).

15. Dennis Rondinelli, "Financing the Decentralization of Urban Services in Developing Countries: Administrative Requirements for Fiscal Improvements," *Studies in Comparative International Development* (Summer 1990), 53.

16. Oxford Analytica, Ltd., *Role of the Public Sector in Latin America,* 66.

17. World Bank, *Argentina: Public Finance Review, From Insolvency to Growth* (Washington, D.C.: World Bank, 1993), 43.

18. World Bank, *Ecuador Public Expenditure Review: Changing the Role of the State* (Washington, D.C.: World Bank, 1993). Ironically, Ecuador was one of the few Latin American countries to increase its infrastructural maintenance expenditures during the 1980s. This fact underscores the inadequacy of the base from which many countries will have to begin their improvements.

19. Rogério L.F. Werneck, "Market Failure, Government Failure and Wretched Statecraft: Lessons from the Brazilian Vicious Circle" (paper prepared for the Carlos Diaz-Alejandro Memorial Colloquium on "Latin America in the 1990s" sponsored by the Inter-American Development Bank, Washington, D.C., 6 May 1993).

20. World Bank, *Peru: Poverty Assessment and Social Policies and Programs for the Poor* (Washington, D.C.: World Bank, 1993), 28.

21. Oxford Analytica, Ltd., *Role of the Public Sector in Latin America,* 91.

22. Rondinelli, "Financing the Decentralization of Urban Services," 51.

23. See Sebastian Edwards, "Economic Reform, Labor Markets and the Social Sectors: A Latin American Perspective" (unpublished manuscript, World Bank, Washington, D.C., 1993).